sugar
love poems

poems, body, design
by M. CANTO

Note for Librarians: A cataloguing record for this book is available from Library and Archives Canada at www.collectionscanada.ca/amicus/index-e.html
ISBN 1-4120-4953-9

Printed in Victoria, BC, Canada. Printed on paper with minimum 30% recycled fibre. Trafford's print shop runs on "green energy" from solar, wind and other environmentally-friendly power sources.

TRAFFORD

Offices in Canada, USA, Ireland and UK

This book was published *on-demand* in cooperation with Trafford Publishing. On-demand publishing is a unique process and service of making a book available for retail sale to the public taking advantage of on-demand manufacturing and Internet marketing. On-demand publishing includes promotions, retail sales, manufacturing, order fulfilment, accounting and collecting royalties on behalf of the author.

Book sales for North America and international:
Trafford Publishing, 6E–2333 Government St.,
Victoria, BC v8t 4p4 CANADA
phone 250 383 6864 (toll-free 1 888 232 4444)
fax 250 383 6804; email to orders@trafford.com
Book sales in Europe:
Trafford Publishing (uk) Ltd., Enterprise House, Wistaston Road Business Centre,
Wistaston Road, Crewe, Cheshire cw2 7rp UNITED KINGDOM
phone 01270 251 396 (local rate 0845 230 9601)
facsimile 01270 254 983; orders.uk@trafford.com
Order online at:
trafford.com/04-2761

10 9 8 7 6 5 4 3

dear Toni, Spunky Sister

Stay Beautiful,
Stay Sexy

♡
m. _____

Aug. 2009

contents

contents

contents

contents

M. Canto lives in Melbourne. She has been published in Australian magazines including the nationals *The Weekend Australian, Quadrant and australianreader.com*, and engaged at various times as journalist, radio dj, singer-songwriter, dancer, actor, artist's model.

Peter Matulich photographed M. Canto for this project. Peter's photographic works have been exhibited in Australia and featured in *Black&White* magazine.

sugar merges M. Canto's work as poet and muse.

thank you lovers, mothers, fathers, friends, punters

for anyone who's ever loved

SUGAR

take me
very
slowly.
like smoking
a cigar
or budding
like a flower.

ORAL

it begins with
the mouth.
beautiful blue smile,
beautiful while.

SEXY

poetry is not
dead. it's sexy.
it turns me on like
you and me speechless
when we understand our mouths
get in the way of what we
really want to say.

INCLINATION

i shall caress
the total mess
you are and kiss
your inclination to un-impress
me with your careless-
ness.

HELLO

my last lover's name was
Michelangelo, like yours.
which, next to mine,
on paper, looked good. side
by side your name and mine swell
with the journalism of my yellow
spanish shoes disturbing
your very straight jacket.
do you smoke?

TOUCH ME

touch me as if
you were blind: feeling
with the eyes of your hand
every part of my meaning.
finding the truth.
and lingering.

WHAT IS A BRA

what is a bra but a piece
of wire, lace
string teasing
you into untying
me. it is not modesty.
untying's the thing. why,
i would put on the bra
i do not wear
for untying's sake to remind
you you are privileged
to unstrap me,
to know me bare,
to go beyond this cleavage
that entices because
i don't live in the same house
as you, that is all.

PICTURE

boys. i like them when
they're different. when
they're not indifferent.
when i put it on gorgeous
and they call
me all manner of doll
things. but i don't promise
anything. not everything
again. today i live
forever young:
my mother is not me,
a roll of film in spring,
the flower flowering, coming
like Princess Red.

AS BUTTER

to lubricate, caress.
caress and kiss her face,
her neck, her ears,
her back, her breasts,
her feet, her thighs,
and lie with her a little undone,
not thoroughly, never
totally, to begin.

continued

whisper her
beautiful-ness,
your truthfulness
or soft meaninglessness,
your fullness
with her tenderness.
and she'll be
in your hands as honey,
as dough, as butter.

now undo her absolutely.
and hear her cry.

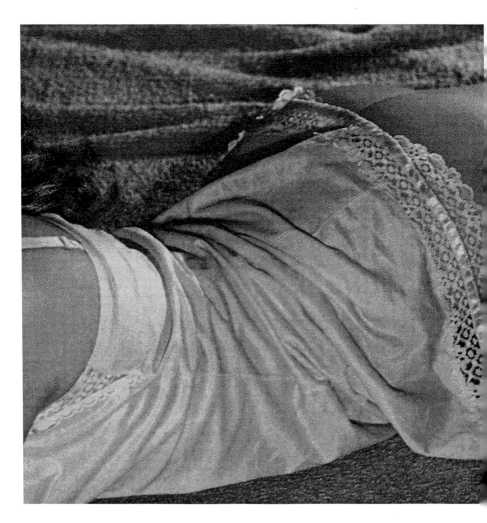

WILD

you are beautiful, God
Bless You, he said when
he meant i was wild
to not care about my hair bigger
than my face, smaller
than my breasts in his hands.

SCARED

i was afraid
of this: missing
you from kissing
you.

NOW

now memory
does not satisfy.
now imagination
will not melt words in
my mouth. my lines are
weak, i play with speech where
letters and their accents won't
repeat what really went
between us when we kissed.

THE BODY

until last night
i hadn't tasted
anything outside
The Body of Christ.
and oh i must
confess i am converted.

CHARITY

this is my body.
will my charity
begin and end with the donation
of my organs to the dying when
i am dead?

I WOULD NOT BLUSH

i would not blush
were i mere animal.
so my red hush
in court proclaims me criminal,
my crime being: being
in love with you. witness
my crimson face telling,
gushing wordless
about you who pleases
me and whom i long
to please.

ANIMAL

prey on me tonight.
i have watched
you panting
after my meat,
pretending nothing.
i was just as
hungry, feigning
anorexia. didn't i say
i was jealous
of the moon's fatness
when it was full?
tonight let the big moon
in the forest
catch us.

ENGLISH LOVE

above love there is no
other. we know.
straight-
A glass-eye boy's late
for english
class with fish-
eye curly girl. english teacher
curls her english tongue. father
loves mother
large with me, sister and brother.
loves mother's
morning face and gown and hair. mother cares
for me and sister's sameness,
for brother's difference.

continued

we speak
love in english. we are weak
in love. straight-
A boy and english teacher twist-
ed english tongue for
love of english. mother and father bore
you and me and sister
and brother
high in love. so we show straight-A
boy and english teacher. we say hey,
father, mother, sister, brother, look,
we love each other. we want the english book.
we read and speak the english body
language. we
move our mouths, our tongues, our eyes,
our arms and rise
and fall over the other.
mother, father: meet my english lover.

I WISH

i wish
i too
had your dress's
access
to you.

CERTAINLY

certainly as the nails on my toes are painted
with your interpretation
of forgiveness, you can sin
swiftly with me with the simplicity of steamed
rice.

SOFT

i feel this way
about you: soft.

i cried
when they cut the cord
that contained our conversations
and the record
of our pulses. substitutes
for you distracted before
this stillness before me.

this softness is
our evidence.

DIRTY

your hands are filthy
with the manness i want
against my womanhood. touch
my silk china dirty, mark it
with the distinction of used things.

CONVERSATION

his mouth found mine
again, found my beginning,
my cream in between.
only my mouth pleased
his, only his eyes pleased
mine. we pulled
and pushed this way
and that, extraordinary
blood pumping hearts
pounding mouths eating
eyes burning skin brushing
dress and everything
flesh consuming flesh
undressed, glowing.
and when all was said
between us, i screamed.

GREASE

your leather jacket
has eaten me. consumed me
so i no longer
remember things besides
meeting you
in a packed, merry place
run by mechanical
strangers.

you threw me
in your black, open
car, smelt the leather
of my shoes.

continued

i threw out my feet
like my hands and we were one
rebellious parade down
money street.

the gas station
shook when we stepped on its grease-
circles and danced because
the moon was as full
of milk as we.

GIRL

and they recorded in the baby book
everything the baby girl, child of love,
was: lips of her mother, nose of both, eyes
of her father. the woman and the man
studied the girl in her pink pillow dress
and smiled. and dreamt of her first walk and talk.

of their first child, much study, dreaming, talk,
adoration. all in the baby book
was recorded. baby's first cry, first dress,
first kiss, first smile. the first child (girl) of love
of the woman and the man made the man
proud of the woman's lips, proud of his eyes.

continued

the man's eyes were big and brown. the girl's eyes
followed his. the girl's lips parted in talk
like her mother's. the woman watched the man
watch the girl grow, read their first child the book,
read her book dreams, names and ways of things, love
the girl like he loved the woman. her dress

of pink, of crimson roses, pretty dress
of her childhood is now the child's. big eyes
talk as pink lips close: talk of names of love,
ways of love, love-book dreams and things. love-talk
of eyes now read in dreams and words of book
and part of lips. the woman and the man

continued

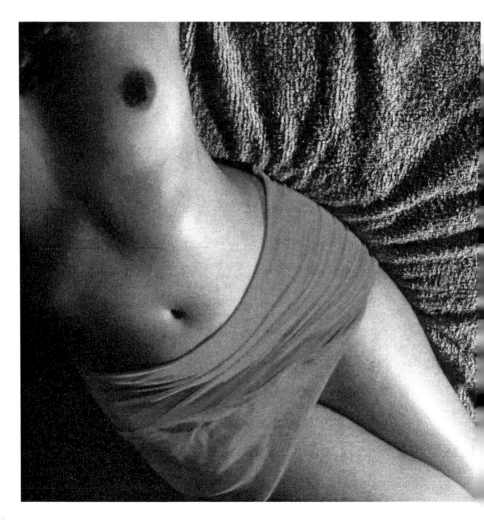

watch the girl grow. now the girl loves the man
and the woman but is proud of her dress.
the man does not read the big girl the book
now because she can read with her big eyes,
dream what she reads, read and dream more than talk
to the woman and the man about love.

the woman and the man know about love,
read in words of love-book and dreams: some man
will love the girl, will listen to her talk,
will watch her walk, will love her in rose dress,
love her pink lips, read love in her big eyes.
the girl is a dream-girl in the love-book.

the woman and the man read in the book
of love dreams the girl recorded. big eyes
talk, say: some man loves the girl in rose dress.

TODAY

today i am in your best
red dress pressed,
caressed, caressing.
warm, i warm.

as the dancer's,
so is my spine
tender.

the sun, my god,
is in your eyes
like lightning splitting
black.

you are most
moved by poetry.

MY GOD

alone i know i love you
more than this piercing
quiet, so necessary
to see i need you suddenly
like God to explain
the unexplainable, this
more than whiff of heaven.

continued

i have been looking
at Jesus' face with eyes
that look through me for years: my god,
you look like him. my god
has come to life. face to face
with you who knows everything
i am is the meaning
of stoned. i shut up. i feel: my god,
the mystery. you kiss my feet.

YOU

you have become
everywhere: this splash of apple
on my bottled run on the asphalt
with the multi-drops of sun
dissolving into your face now taking
all queens' and all presidents'
places in my trading
money. i'm buying into the famous
subject of tv news
and sales you have become:
omnipresent and unmistakable.
unnecessary, even, as
American pie in Russia. yet
there you are.

THEREFORE

therefore do not
marry me, do not live
with me. i might
become your sister
or your mother
whose breasts you sucked
from need or watched
covered, scared of you that
had become the man they could not
bathe with now unashamed.
i will be honest
with you. but not familiar.

NOTE

forgive me for stealing
your dress while you were sleeping.
but i will
miss you and want to fill
your dress with your picture.
i will hold it and remember
our dances. and remember to return
for mine.

SOMETHING

there is something
about you, before me, dressed:
the throbbing in my head
uncovering you unknowing.
you, before me, not seeing
my hands have moved,
fulfilling in explicit pictures this almighty
push to get to your absolute
nothing-on beautiful.

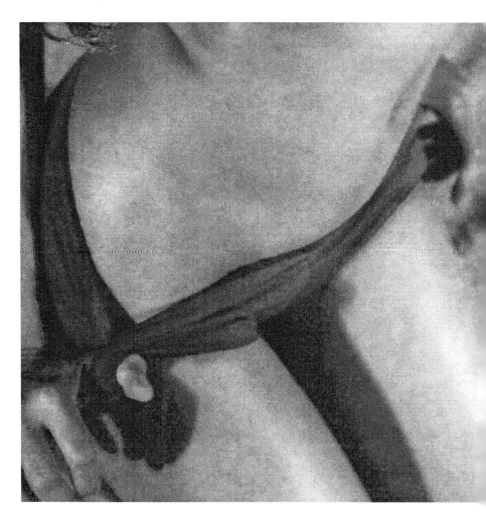

PLEASE

would you please
drop the nonsense
and dismiss
your dress?

CONCERT

then i could no longer
play the piano. my fingers
died to hand and mouth
arrangements you ran down
my back extemporaneous,
unsheeted.

and jazz was
never sexier.

REPLY TO A PROPOSITION

if you must
love me, love me
like my dress kisses
my self-possession.

and i shall wear
you infinitely proud
where it flatters most.

YESTERDAY

yesterday the song
you wrote and sang
for me tore through my dress.
and there i was again
with you. in dearest spaces
in certain rooms and streets
and trains and cars.
your smell in my hair,
my bed, my skin.
my mouth pressed
on your chest, sweet mouth
on your belly and below.

continued

.

pink skies and purple
flowers fell on us
in your mother's garden
where we got scared because
we'd touched the holy
grail. jesus, what if
it slipped and broke?
we ran away from the all-
beautiful, all-blinding thing
thinking it undeserved.
but we were perfect
then.

ABSENT

holy camera of my head.
blessed memory that freezes
the details of the pictures,
the sounds, the scents, the tastes,
the everything of you. the visible
invisible, more concrete than all
concrete things: your love's
more present here now that you're
nowhere with me.

ONE THING

to say that you&me
are merely two
is true only
to the material eye.

one thing i am afraid
of losing: our hearts
to the much exact non-flowers
of a limiting mathematics.

EVERYTHING

strip me
of extra. love
me. strip you
of extra. love
me. extra, extra,
everything else
is extra.
eat my jewellery.
love me.
love me more
than accessory.

THAT

that i were child again
and nevermore squander paper and pen
but tell you as i did then
say simply i love you, Ben.

UTTER LOVE

i don't speak
your mother tongue,
you don't speak
mine. we love us most
when we don't
speak together.
we love us most
when we don't speak.
please don't translate.
and i won't consult
the book of love translated.
love is best
not understood.

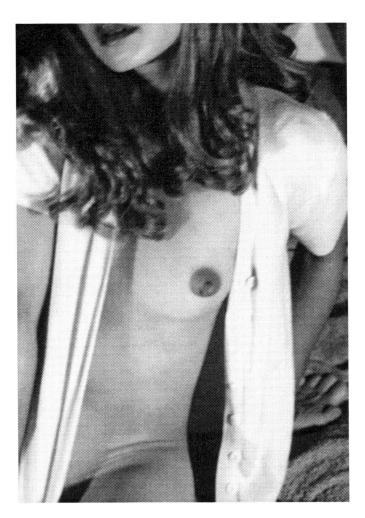

BLACK&WHITE

i cannot love you more
than this page of words that will stay
long after i forget the slant
of your face. it will weaken
me with unblinking black
and white stares: the naked
strength of the truth
of our moments.

THEN

i will find the words
for this gut desire.
i will paint this whiteness
with them that feel like
pictures you've always
wanted to see. and see
and see again.
because they will taste
the taste your true tongue's
been denied.

continued

they will seize
the moment of truth,
the moment of love,
and freeze them
and give them
as blood to the white-livered
and the living dead.
and they get a grip
on what it all means.
then, i will die.

CRY

your sweat is
sweet to my sense
of smell, my sense
of touching tears
not from your eyes.
you say you should be clean
when your skin
crying bitter all over
me is my utmost sense
of taste, my overriding water-
slide.

WICKED

untie your hair. i like
the way it gets confused
with mine, the way we get
confused in this wicked
mess, sure about the way
we fit, about the way
only you can confine me.

SUNDAY

sunday holy sunday.
all day all things outside
us be hanged: the cat,
the paper, the invitation to the opening
of the mouth of sir/madam something,
the sun. forget my monday
speech to save somebody
else's ass. sunday we return
to heaven, to honesty, to the time
before we sinned,
when we were unpunished, undressed.
sunday i love you like new,
love only you, love and love you
within and without these sheets.
you forgive me, i forgive you
sunday. all day we are divine
ruling again: man and woman
naked, present, perfect.

CLEARLY

it is very difficult to mark
your eyes in the dark
and place you properly.

your proper place is
clearly before my eyes,
your first place of becoming to me
everything else i cannot see.

i must love you in the light.
i cannot take for granted
perfect sight.

AGAIN

repeat yourself
to me, you who pledged allegiance
to my breasts: retie
them to your tongue,
recover this skin's bareness
with your own,
swear in my ear again,
once more honour
my honour.

SCREAMING

take me away
one day fast. screaming
red, i'd ride and ride
and ride with you.
so electric wind
in my hair, so perfect heaven
weather, i could not care.
i could rear my head.
so electric up and down,
round and round
we'd go fast screaming
red. so perfect heaven
weather, so electric
wind in my hair, oh red
electric fast heaven,
i could not screaming
care.

BOMBSHELL

men's eyes explode
before my skin, coincide
with concussions in my brain
that must contain
warring attractions,

persuasions primal fighting
my soul's senses.

tick, tick, tick, tick.
DETONATE. KILL.

kill time and men
with raw distraction.

LOVE IS

look at the candle,
darling: like you&me -
the wick and the wax burning
with the other, explaining
love.

50,000 burning
hours would spill love's juice
round that wine
bottle, testifying:
love is art.

ELSEWHERE

elsewhere love
is happening while
you and i, we
think too much.

MEET YOU

see the sun rise, see
it unhurried fit flaming
in the centre of the universe.
tonight i will meet you
like the sun.

SUCKER

we meet at your kitchen
table like knife and fork unwitting, moving
food to mouth in civil eating.
my body is fed with more
than bread. my life comes
from what's in your head, feeding
me past the emptiness of plates, i am:
full before they're empty, sucker
for mind-blowing things.

COFFEE

they ordered coffee. he ordered for her
and him. she had chocolate, not coffee
(she did not drink coffee). the cake menu
was tempting. he liked the way her v-neck
dress showed a part of her he was curious
about. she felt his eyes and became red

in white parts, red looked like pink instead. Red
was the name of the place. she picked out her
cake. he pretended to take a curious-
ity to the Red cake display. coffee
would come soon, said a merry waiter, neck
collared in Red fashion, white menu

continued

dressing red belt. Red red belt. the menu
was taken away. her parts that were red
had returned to normal. he touched the neck
of the Red-mannered glass of water her
tongue had touched before, before the coffee
finally came. he asked where the curious

-looking cup had come from. she was curious.
the merry waiter said some place, menu
at the Red was discussed before coffee
and chocolate were consumed. they'd turned red
from the fireplace heat. she thought she'd tie her
hair back. this worked her hands and freed her neck.

continued

she smiled a certain way, touching her neck,
looking at the cup (again) so curious,
thinking perhaps what to say. he made her
laugh about something. i read the menu,
read the paper, consumed my coffee. Red
was known for its chocolate and coffee

unlike any other. to have coffee
at the Red was also curious. the neck
of stringed instruments collared in the Red
manner, exhibited, dressed by curious
thoughts of people on paper, was menu
besides coffee and chocolate. now her

cake was consumed also. he looked at her.
they looked happy, quite pleased with the menu.
they saw me look at them. i was curious.

SIMPLE

the look on my face
today is enviable, as
if i did not curse the economics
of the government
of the day or God at night
for not making me inanimate
and insensitive.
after all, to blush
pretty and be loved by you is
simplest.

BLOOD

you will surrender
when i say i want lip
service. i mean: read
my lips. they are the colour
of your blood. of any man's
alive. and man and man
will shoot each other dead
with gun when i put on
my lipstick. these lips
are news: blood-red
they drip and you drop dead
and everybody cries murder
when it was suicide, lips
out of synch.

DEAD

this is useless, this
fight to find the right
words to bring you to life.
beside me are words
and words i cannot hold
and cannot eat for want.
they do not resurrect
you. he lied who said
they could for they are dead
in my hands: unforming
your likeness, deforming
you. vain pile of words
better slashed, conspiring
against me, howling this
unshakeable longing, this
stark wanting nothing
else but you.

HERE

my favourite place
is still in your arms. there i lose
most every care. it is as if the world
made difficult by man unbacked
by grace to run it is nil.
and our simple still
says we have most power
here.

THE END

the end of the purpose
of my pen has come
with your coming.
i am staring at a blank
page, you are staring
at me. you who i merely
imagined once, you:
the substance of my words
before me now turning
my skin, my hair, my mind,
my heart to wax to construct
as you please. you:
to whom i've lost my contract
to compose.

KIND OF

love is this kind of
moon-peaceful.
an electric decision
to touch. the wild
blue striking from
the universe's freedom
centre, flooding
the loved with nerve.
the fragrance
of garments just
powder-beaten.

BELIEVE

believe me,
poet with this love
proposition, least.
my love is never
fairer than my eloquences
that seep through your
affections as night breeze
or sweet music and negotiate
you like a yo-yo. that this
dense poverty of words is
your seduction is my craft,
my licence to kill you
sincerely.

EXPIRY

sooner or later
my body will be worm-eaten
unlike your venerable guitar
that shall never perish in
its mummy-box under your bed
unless one purposeful cigarette
butt makes an arsonist
of you. while i am undead,
use your common sense.

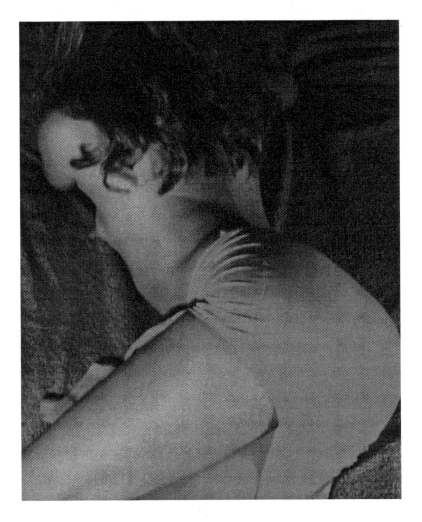